I Can Be Anything!

I CAN BE A DENTIST

By Nancy Greenwood

Please visit our website, www.garethstevens.com. For a free color catalog of all our high-quality books, call toll free 1-800-542-2595 or fax 1-877-542-2596.

Cataloging-in-Publication Data
Names: Greenwood, Nancy.
Title: I can be a dentist / Nancy Greenwood.
Description: New York : Gareth Stevens Publishing, 2021. | Series: I can be anything! | Includes index.
Identifiers: ISBN 9781538255469 (pbk.) | ISBN 9781538255483 (library bound) | ISBN 9781538255476 (6 pack)
Subjects: LCSH: Dentists–Juvenile literature. | Teeth–Care and hygiene–Juvenile literature. | Dentistry–Vocational guidance–Juvenile literature.
Classification: LCC RK63.G737 2021 | DDC 617.6'023–dc23

First Edition

Published in 2021 by
Gareth Stevens Publishing
111 East 14th Street, Suite 349
New York, NY 10003

Editor: Kate Mikoley
Designer: Laura Bowen

Photo credits: Cover, p. 1 (kid) powerofforever/iStock/Getty Images Plus/Getty Images; cover, p.1 (background) anatoliy_gleb/Shutterstock.com; pp. 5, 7, 9, 11, 15, 17, 24 (teeth and X-ray) wavebreakmedia/Shutterstock.com; pp. 13, 24 (floss) luckyraccoon/Shutterstock.com; pp. 19, 21 New Africa/Shutterstock.com; p. 23 Veronica Louro/Shutterstock.com.

Printed in the United States of America

CPSIA compliance information: Batch #CS20GS: For further information contact Gareth Stevens, New York, New York at 1-800-542-2595.

Contents

Dr. Kay is a dentist.
She looks at my mouth.

I sit in a big chair!

Dr. Kay cleans my teeth.
She uses special tools.

She taught me to brush.

I use floss too.
It looks like string!

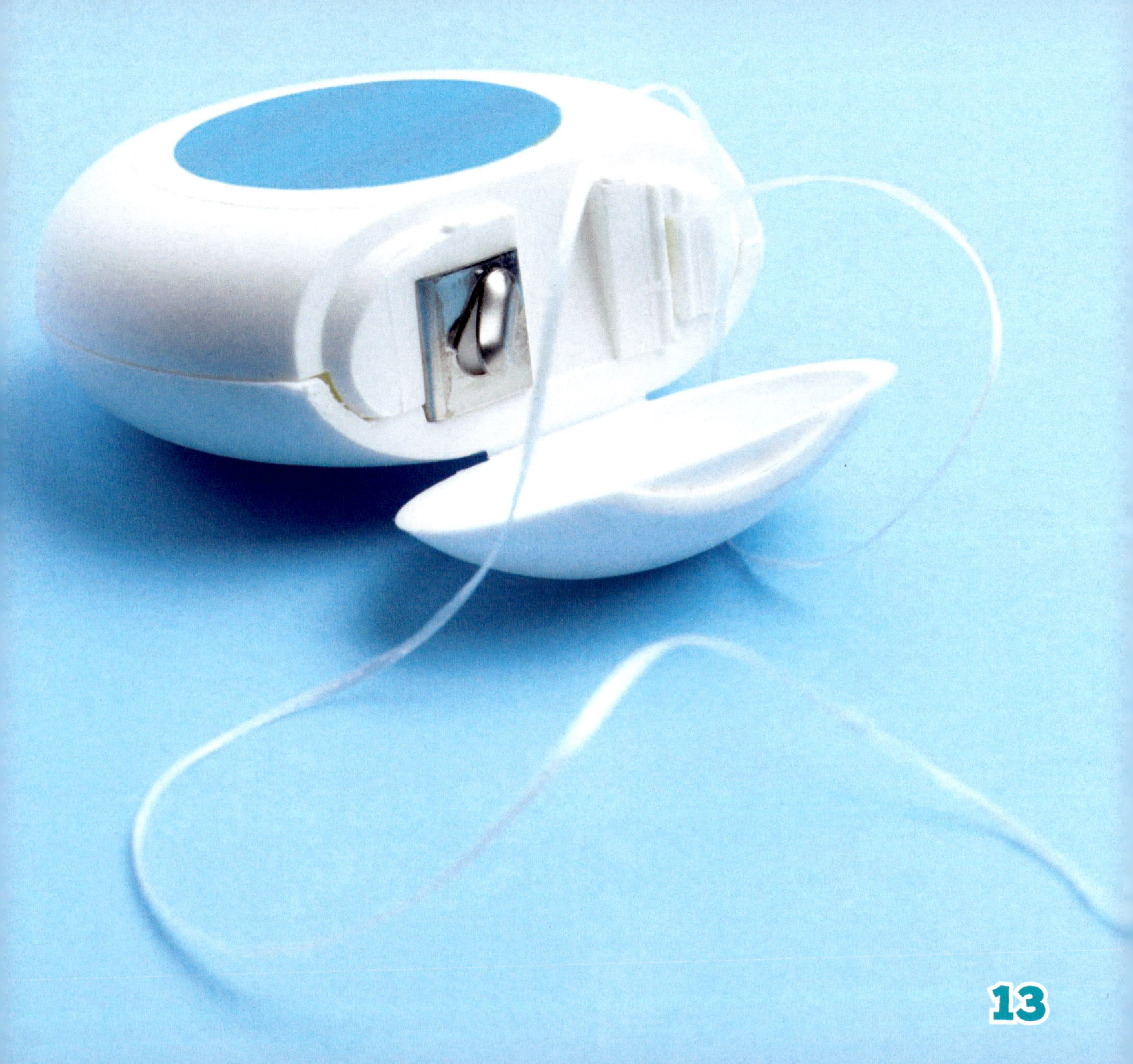

We take X-rays.
They see what we can't!

Dr. Kay says my teeth look great!

You may get a cavity.
This is a hole in a tooth.

A dentist can fix it.

I can be a dentist.
So can you!

Words to Know

floss

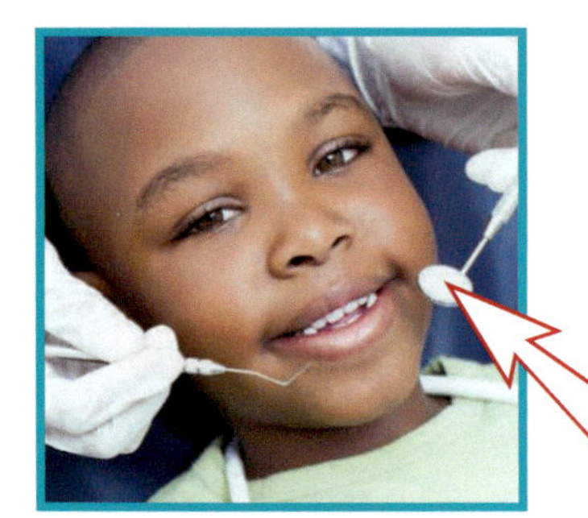

tools

X-ray

Index